ELEPHANTS

by Jenny Markert

Content Adviser:
The Zoological Society
of San Diego

Published in the United States of America by The Child's World®
PO Box 326 • Chanhassen, MN 55317-0326
800-599-READ • www.childsworld.com

PHOTO CREDITS
© Adam Jones/Dembinsky Photo Associates: 6–7
© Andy Rouse/Getty: cover, 1
© Anup Shah/Animals Animals–Earth Scenes: 10
© Art Wolfe/Getty: 14–15, 25
© Corbis: 21
© Daniel J. Cox/naturalexposures.com: 20
© Galen Rowell/Corbis: 5
© Gerald Hinde/Getty: 19
© Mark J. Thomas/Dembinsky Photo Associates: 9
© Martin Harvey/Corbis: 23, 27
© Martin Withers/Dembinsky Photo Associates: 17
© Ronnie Kaufman/Corbis: 28
© Stan Osolinski/Dembinsky Photo Associates: 12

ACKNOWLEDGMENTS
The Child's World®: Mary Berendes, Publishing Director;
Katherine Stevenson, Editor

The Design Lab: Kathleen Petelinsek, Design and Page Production

LIBRARY OF CONGRESS CATALOGING-IN-PUBLICATION DATA
Markert, Jenny.
  Elephants / by Jenny Markert.
     p. cm. — (New naturebooks)
  Includes bibliographical references and index.
  ISBN 1-59296-637-3 (library bound : alk. paper)
  1. Elephants—Juvenile literature. I. Title. II. Series.
  QL737.P98M3692 2006
  599.67—dc22   2006001365

Table of Contents

On the cover: This huge African elephant is walking in South Africa's Marakele National Park.

Meet the Elephant!

Elephants are related to hundreds of elephant-like animals that are now **extinct**. The most recent were mammoths, which died out only about 9,000 years ago.

Today, the closest living relatives of elephants are manatees, dugongs, aardvarks, and hyraxes.

The dry African plain is hot and quiet under the midday sun. Gentle breezes rustle through the grasses and tree branches. All around, animals are grazing or resting in the afternoon heat. One place, however, is full of noise and action. Huge animals are splashing at the water hole, taking their afternoon baths. What animals are causing all this noise? They're elephants!

These two young African elephants are drinking and cooling off in a water hole in Tanzania.

What Do Elephants Look Like?

The skin of an elephant can be up to 1 inch (2.5 cm) thick.

An elephant's skin is so sensitive, it can feel flies and other insects that land on it.

Elephants are the biggest animals that live on land. They have thick, wrinkled gray skin and thin tails. Adult elephants can be nearly as tall as a school bus and weigh as much as four small cars. To support their huge bodies, they have strong, thick legs. Their legs look like moving tree trunks! Each leg is strong enough to support the elephant's whole body. But an elephant's legs aren't made for running or jumping. Elephants usually move slowly. They can't jump even an inch off the ground!

You can see all the wrinkles in this African elephant's skin as it stands in the sunshine.

Are There Different Kinds of Elephants?

African elephants can be found in two types of areas: flat grasslands, called *savannas*, and green forests.

There are only two types of elephants—African elephants and Asian elephants. Both types are named for the parts of the world in which they live. African elephants are bigger. They can grow to be 13 feet (4 m) tall and weigh about 14,000 pounds (6,350 kg). They also have large, floppy ears that cover their necks and shoulders.

This female African elephant is walking across a field with her baby. You can see how thick and wrinkled the adult's skin is, especially on her forehead and trunk.

Asian elephants used to be called Indian elephants. They are smaller than African elephants and have much smaller ears. Asian elephants reach about 10 feet (3 m) in height and weigh about 11,000 pounds (4,990 kg). In many areas where Asian elephants live, people have tamed them to do work. These tame elephants perform jobs that call for a lot of strength, such as hauling logs. Sometimes people even ride them like giant horses!

Asian elephants have two large bumps on the tops of their heads. African elephants do not. Asian elephants also have smoother skin than African elephants.

This adult Asian elephant is standing in a forest in Kanha, India. Compare it to the African elephant photo on page 9. Which elephant has bigger ears?

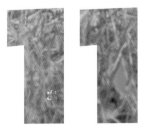

11

All African elephants, both male and female, have two **tusks**. Among Asian elephants, only the males have tusks long enough to see. The tusks are extra-long teeth that grow out of the elephant's mouth. Elephants use their tusks to rip bark off trees or to defend themselves against attackers.

Some elephants' tusks grow very long. In fact, the longest tusk ever measured was over 11 feet (over 3 m) long! Most elephants have one tusk shorter than the other. The shorter tusk is worn down from being used more.

Elephants begin growing tusks when they are about six months old.

Male elephants' tusks are thicker and heavier than females' tusks.

Tusks grow about 7 inches (18 cm) a year. They keep growing as long as the elephant lives.

This male African elephant is walking in a field in eastern Africa. Can you tell which tusk he uses more often?

Do Elephants Live Alone?

Elephants make many different sounds to communicate with each other. People cannot even hear some of these sounds. One type of low, rumbling elephant call can be heard by another elephant up to 5 miles (8 km) away.

Elephants live in family groups called **herds**. Each herd has about 10 to 40 elephants. The elephants in a herd are friendly, loving, and protective with each other. If one elephant gets sick or hurt, the others comfort and protect it. The herds are ruled by female elephants.

Elephants live a **nomadic** life, moving from place to place. They must keep moving to search for food—an adult can eat 100 to 200 pounds (45 to 91 kg) of food in one day! If the herd stayed in one place, the elephants would soon run out of food.

This herd of African elephants is walking in a swampy area in Kenya.

14

What Do Elephants Eat?

Besides their tusks, elephants have four other flat teeth, or molars, that they use for chewing their food. They have two molars on the bottom and two molars on the top.

Elephants are **herbivores**, which means that they eat only plants. Elephants like to munch on tree leaves, bark, and roots. They also eat flowers, bushes, and shrubs. Elephants need so much food that it's hard for them to be picky! When elephants eat, they grab food with their long trunks and pull it into their mouths.

This African elephant is using its trunk to strip bark from a tree. Inside its mouth, you can see its flat molars.

What Is an Elephant's Trunk Like?

An elephant has at least 40,000 different muscles that move its trunk.

An elephant's trunk is heavy! Sometimes an elephant will rest it on a tusk to take a break from carrying it.

Elephants breathe only through their trunks—never through their mouths.

An elephant's trunk is strong, flexible, and made of muscle. It's actually a long nose! It has many uses, but one of its most important jobs is to smell. Elephants have a very good sense of smell. They can smell people from 2 miles (3 km) away and can even smell water underground.

Elephants use their trunks to communicate, too. They grunt and snort through their trunks to talk to each other. If an elephant senses danger, it bangs its trunk on the ground to warn others. Elephants also scare enemies by raising their trunks above their heads and trumpeting loudly.

18

This African elephant has curled its trunk into an S shape. Elephants often raise their trunks this way to smell the surrounding air.

Here you can see the two "fingers" on an African elephant's trunk.

Elephants use their trunks to grab things and pick up food. The end of an African elephant's trunk has two parts that work like fingers. These two parts let the elephant pick up small objects easily. Asian elephants' trunks have only one of these "fingers." Elephants also use their trunks to drink—but not like a straw. Instead, the elephant sucks water into its trunk and then sprays the water into its mouth.

One trunkful of water is about 1 to 2 gallons (4 to 8 liters). An adult elephant drinks about 60 gallons (227 liters) a day.

An elephant swimming in deep water uses its trunk as a snorkel. The elephant's body might be completely underwater, but the trunk stays above the water so the elephant can breathe.

This close-up picture shows how elephants grasp short grasses. They curl their trunks around a clump of grass and pull. The whole clump is ripped from the ground, and the elephant can then enjoy a tasty snack.

What Are Baby Elephants Like?

Elephants are mammals, which means they have warm bodies and feed their babies milk from their bodies.

Female elephants are able to have babies until they are about 50 years old.

Just as some human babies suck their thumbs, some elephant calves suck on their trunks.

Female elephants, called *cows,* give birth to just one baby at a time. The baby, called a *calf,* weighs about 200 pounds (91 kg) when it is born. It can stand up when it is only a few hours old. For the first few years, the calf stays close to its mother. At first, it drinks only the milk the mother makes in her body. Over time, the calf learns how to eat grasses and shrubs. It also learns how to stay safe by watching its mother and the other elephants in the herd.

22

This young African elephant calf is sniffing the air in Amboseli National Reserve. The reserve is a protected area in the nation of Kenya and covers 1,260 square miles (3,263 sq km).

How Do Elephants Stay Safe?

Elephants also use their ears to cool themselves in hot weather. When they fan their ears back and forth, air passing over the ears' blood vessels cools the elephant's blood.

Hungry animals such as wild dogs, lions, or hyenas sometimes eat baby elephants that wander away from the herd. But few animals are brave enough to attack a whole herd of elephants—or even just one adult! When danger is near, the adults bunch together around the herd's weaker and younger members. When the enemies leave, the elephants return to eating and playing.

African elephants have a secret weapon for scaring away enemies—their ears! When African elephants stick out their huge ears, they look even bigger than they really are. Other animals would rather go away hungry than risk getting squashed by such a huge elephant.

24

Here you can see an angry African elephant as it watches the photographer in Namibia. It has flared its ears to appear even bigger—a warning sign that the photographer should keep away!

Are Elephants in Danger?

Elephants can live to be about 70 years old.

Illegal hunters called poachers often kill all the adults in a herd. Then the baby elephants have no older animals to show them where to find water or where to travel.

Unfortunately, the elephant's size doesn't frighten away people. Countless elephants have been hunted and killed for their tusks. The tusks are made of **ivory**, a valuable substance used to make jewelry, art, and piano keys. Killing so many wild elephants has caused both African and Asian elephants to become **endangered**—in danger of becoming extinct.

This Asian elephant lives in a protected area, where hunting is illegal. Outside of the protected area, this elephant would probably be killed for its valuable tusks.

Over the years, many people have come to understand the need to protect elephants. Countries have begun to ban killing elephants for ivory. But the elephants face another problem. Farming and building have destroyed many of the elephants' **habitats**, or living areas. Elephants cannot live without large areas in which to eat, sleep, and raise their babies. Some countries are creating special parks where elephants can live safely. If we can give elephants a safe place to live, these amazing animals will be around for thousands of years to come.

Elephants are very important to other animals. They pull down trees, dig water-holes, and create trails. Other animals use these forest openings, waterholes, and trails.

Elephants are very smart animals. They use sticks and rocks as tools, they have excellent memories, and they even show sadness when a herd member dies.

This African elephant and her baby are walking at sunset. The rest of their herd is following nearby.

Glossary

endangered (en-DANE-jerd) Endangered animals are animals that are in danger of dying out. Elephants are endangered.

extinct (eks-TINKT) When an animal becomes extinct, it means that there are no more of them left alive. Mammoths, an ancient relative of today's elephants, are extinct.

habitat (HAB-ih-tat) An animal's habitat is the type of place or environment in which it lives. Building and farming have destroyed many of the elephant's habitats.

herbivores (HER-bih-vohrz) Herbivores are animals that eat only plant foods, not meat. Elephants are herbivores.

herds (HERDZ) Herds are groups of animals that live together. Elephants live in family herds of up to 40 animals.

ivory (EYE-vree) An elephant's tusks are made of white ivory that can be carved into many shapes. Many elephants have been killed for their ivory.

mammals (MAM-ullz) Mammals are animals that have warm bodies and feed their babies milk from their bodies. Elephants and people are both mammals.

molars (MOH-lurz) Molars are flat teeth used for grinding food. Elephants have four molars in their mouths.

nomadic (noh-MAD-ik) Nomadic means moving from place to place rather than settling in one spot. Elephant herds are nomadic.

poachers (POH-churz) Poachers are people who hunt illegally. Elephants have been victims of poachers for many years.

tusks (TUSKS) Tusks are very long teeth that grow out of an elephant's mouth. Elephant tusks are several feet long.

To Find Out More

Watch It!

Reflections on Elephants. VHS. Washington, DC: National Geographic Society, 1994.

The Ultimate Guide—Elephants. VHS. Bethesda, MD: Discovery Channel Video, 1998.

Read It!

Kalman, Bobbie. *Endangered Elephants.* New York: Crabtree, 2005.

MacMillan, Dianne M. *Elephants: Our Last Land Giants.* Minneapolis, MN: Carolrhoda, 1993.

Redmond, Ian. *Elephant.* New York: Dorling Kindersley, 2000.

Smith, Alexander McCall and LeUyen Pham (illustrator). *Akimbo and the Elephants.* New York: Bloomsbury Children's Books, 2005.

Sobol, Richard. *An Elephant in the Backyard.* New York: Dutton Children's Books, 2004.

On the Web

Visit our home page for lots of links about elephants:
http://www.childsworld.com/links

Note to Parents, Teachers, and Librarians: We routinely check our Web links to make sure they're safe, active sites—so encourage your readers to check them out!

Index

About the Author

Jenny Markert lives in Minneapolis, Minnesota, with her husband Mark and children, Hailey and Henry. She is a freelance writer and high- school American literature teacher who loves traveling and adventure in all forms, whether it's sailing the lake on a windy day, hiking the trails by moonlight, or helping her kids learn to boogie board when visiting the ocean. She is an animal lover and an environmentalist who believes, like the great American naturalist Henry David Thoreau, that "in wilderness is the preservation of the world." She is currently working on her second novel.